I'M BRITISH !

BUT IT'S NOT ALWAYS A 'BLACK AND WHITE' ISSUE

by

BIZ LABI

INTRODUCTION

I have written this book because I have not come across anything on the subject of what actually identifies a person as being British in our present time. Although Great Britain is a multicultural nation, there are still issues surrounding a person's identity and questions about their loyalty to Britain, particularly if they are of non-white lineage, and have particular religious affiliations. I myself happen to be the son of immigrants from West Africa, who settled in the United Kingdom back in the 1960s. I felt therefore, that I needed to share my views on this topic, coming directly from a black man who was born and raised in London and how this has affected and shaped my way of thinking. In addition, this book can serve as a voice for the many thousands who have found, and still find themselves facing similar challenges, but have conceded to the pressures of society to never speak out and confront such issues head on.

The United States of America has always had its own issues of racism and inequality towards descendants of immigrants. What we see today in the media only confirms to the rest of the world that there is still a long way to go to solving this problem in the United States. This book highlights similar grievances that we in the United Kingdom are experiencing, albeit on a lower scale. It has even reached a point where recently, 52% of the British population voted to leave the European Union due to what they perceive as a gradual 'take-over' of their ancestral land and an erosion of their values as a result of what they view as an 'open-door immigration policy.' Hopefully, the reader will be able to clearly identify with these issues and acknowledge that this is not simply an American problem, but rather, it remains a problem of the modern Western world.

Table of Contents

Immigration to the United Kingdom of Great Britain

I was born in London in the late 1960s to parents who had migrated to the United Kingdom from the West Coast of Africa. At that time, many of the blacks in Britain had arrived in the 1950s and 1960s from the Caribbean Islands, with a significant number also having arrived from the former British colonies of West Africa. There was a large Southern Asian community that had settled in many parts of the UK. They were mostly of Pakistani, Bangladeshi and Indian origin. Thousands of Ugandan Asians also arrived in the 1970s due to political instability in Uganda.

In the 1970s, if you were to have driven across London, you would undoubtedly have come across ethnically segregated communities which reflected British society at that time. As a young boy, growing up in a middle-class area of South London, I attended a primary school that reflected the community I grew up in, which so happened to be a mixture of blacks and whites. The majority of blacks were of Caribbean origin, whilst there were a few who were of West African descent. Areas, such as Brixton, on the other hand, were classified as 'deprived' areas and were not as ethnically diverse. It was made up of mostly blacks with very few whites. It shot to the headlines in 1981 due to the heavy rioting that took place following a stand-off between the police and the Brixton community. At that time, I couldn't quite pin-point exactly what the cause of the riots were, but all I knew was that black people were fed up with the poor conditions that they had been living in and the inequality and injustice that they had been receiving for so many years at the hands of the system. Tensions reached boiling point and the community felt that they had had enough. What was normally viewed and accepted as just routine police harassment was now going to take another turn and the situation was to spiral out of control. Heavy rioting broke out and lasted for two days in April 1981. It was said that there were up to five thousand people involved, with several injuries on both sides and many arrests. The aftermath left Britain in a state of shock.

I remember during the 1970s, there were areas of London which I would not have dared dream of venturing into, for fear of what I could be met with from the local white residents. Britain was clearly segregated along racial and economic grounds. For the white indigenous population, it was a matter of 'self preservation'. Blacks were not seen as depicting or representing 'British values', so therefore, they were not welcome within British society as a whole. I remember being told of that all-familiar sign that used to be hung up outside the doors of houses or apartments for rent. The sign would clearly spell out, 'No blacks, No dogs, No Irish'. One could conclude that at that time, being British was clearly a 'Black and White' issue.

Moving on into the 1990s and the 2000s, Britain saw a huge influx of immigrants from around the globe. There were many from Africa, Southern Asia, the Middle East and even Europe. The reasons for this immigration varied from country to country and from continent to continent. A lot of it boiled down to shear economic factors. However, there was a significant number that had fled wars in their home countries. Britain had now become even more diverse and more segregated, but this time, there was an added element - religion. Muslims from many parts of Africa and the Middle East poured into Britain to escape conflict and persecution. It was precisely during the period of the 1st Gulf War in 1990, that I myself became a Muslim. At that time, you would hardly ever have seen a Black Muslim anywhere in London. The only Muslims that I did come across were of Southern Asian background. However, as time passed, I began to notice a large presence of black African Muslims from Somalia and Eritrea. I also began to notice Muslims from the Arab world, such as Iraq, Egypt, Morocco and Algeria. Each group had its story for fleeing to the UK. Some accounts spoke of war and terror, whilst others spoke of economic goals and aspirations. The main point is, all of these communities started to reside in areas where they felt that their needs would be best met. For example, Whitechapel, in East London, saw an influx of Somalians and other Muslims from Africa who joined the already existing Bangladeshi community. The local white population felt threatened by this ever-increasing number of Muslims into an area that they saw was their territory. This often led to violent exchanges between both communities - the white British and the Muslim immigrants. It was no longer a 'Black and White' issue anymore, but rather, it was a case of, 'We don't want any other religion in the

UK!' The whites had now found a new enemy that did not share their values and could therefore <u>never</u> be considered as 'British'.

The emergence of radical white groups in the UK

Back in the 1970s there was a radical white-supremacist political party that had neo-Nazi links to it. This group was called the National Front (NF). Although it was established in 1967, it gained prominence in the 1970s due to it winning 20% of the votes in a local election in a city called Leicester, back in 1976. In my view, this group could be considered as the American equivalent of the Klu Klux Klan (KKK). Membership was for whites only and they were bitterly opposed to immigration. Growing up as a child on the streets of London, I remember seeing 'NF' stickers and graffiti everywhere, on walls, on buses, on trains. Fortunately, I never had any personal encounters with any of their sympathisers or supporters. However, there were many less fortunate individuals who gave their accounts of fierce battles that took place between them and supporters of the National Front. Elders within the black community spoke of how they had to engage in bloody encounters just to ward off the random but frequent attacks that they would often experience. Many of us blacks believe that we owe a lot to our elders who stood their ground and paved the way for the younger black generation to always fight back and never give in to injustice and oppression.

As I mentioned towards the end of the previous section, there was a growing resentment towards a new enemy – the Muslims. As a Black Muslim myself, it was easy for me to identify with this new phenomenon that was unfolding around me. I was well acquainted with being targeted for the colour of my skin, or being discriminated against at work, but this was something that had an added dimension to it. It was something intriguing. Blacks were no longer the focus of attention anymore. Their 'Britishness' or loyalty to Britain was no longer in question. They were no longer considered as the enemy, but rather, it was just your mere affiliation to Islam that brought you right into the firing line. It was this new wave of immigrants that had to feel the wrath of the indigenous white population. This gave rise to new radical white-supremacist groups such as the BNP (British National Party), the EDL (English Defence League), and UKIP (United Kingdom Independence Party). Although these parties were all formed at different times, from between the 1980s and 2000s, they all had something in common. Their ideology was similar and it became increasingly noticeable by the 1990s and 2000s. They were all deeply frustrated at what they perceived was a gradual erosion of British values. The irony was that their focus was not primarily on keeping Britain purely 'white' anymore, as they once propagated in their early days. Rather, it was about keeping Britain free of the new emerging religion – Islam. It wasn't a case of 'Black versus White' anymore and it definitely was not a 'Black or White' issue. These parties took a zero-tolerance approach to the presence of any religion in the UK other than Christianity and as a result, focused all of their energy on attacking and demonising the Muslim community in general. There is absolutely no doubt that all of these parties gained significant support from around the UK as they campaigned against the large influx of refugees from the Middle East and Africa. Many converts to their ideology were convinced that Islam was the main cause of their economic woes and the degradation of British society; that the Muslims had flooded the UK only for economic gain and were at the same time, enforcing their religion on the white Christian population. From my own personal perspective, it was not easy to just simply dismiss what they were saying as 'racism' or 'prejudice'. It was somewhat confusing to me, but the problem was, it was all happening so fast and it was causing so much tension up and down the country. Any event that occurred in other parts of the world, which involved Muslims, would inevitably end up being translated onto the streets of Britain where Muslims would have to defend their ideology and practices against the growing onslaught from these radical groups. As a black person, putting my religion aside for a moment, I was able to empathize to some extent, with the growing fears of the white population. Why was Britain opening up the flood gates to all of these immigrants who were not all refugees? Why were so many of them Muslims? Was Britain really prepared and able to handle such a huge number of immigrants who had a completely different way of life? Then there was the issue of 'integration'. How were these Muslims really going to integrate into a society that was predominantly Christian, but also had a large atheist population who did not wish to have any affiliation to religion whatsoever? The presence of Islam in the UK was undoubtedly going to cause some serious discomfort in many quarters of the population, to say the least. The main problem for the indigenous white population and even some of the blacks who were now starting to join the growing sentiment, was that the 'Muslims' are not afraid to outwardly manifest their religion. This means that Islam is a religion that is practiced openly and in public. Basically, it's in your face, whether you like it or not, and there are many who clearly do not like it and do not want to see any public manifestation of religion. Now I began to really understand. All of these developments that were taking place were clearly a slap in the face to many of the British who saw themselves as the ultimate victims of Britain's foreign policies and immigration laws. These were laws, in their view, that allowed people of other religions to reside in the UK and openly practice their way of life, with total disregard to the views and feelings of the indigenous population. I must say, all of this was very deep and somewhat difficult to digest. However, I could clearly see what their grievances were. Britain was now losing its identity. It was becoming less and less clear as to what being 'British' meant.

What does it mean to be British?

Even though I would refer to myself as being British, there is that level of discomfort that crops up within me if asked where I am from. The reason being is because it depends on who is asking the question and how they intend to deal with me once they have got their answer. For example, if questioned by a black person about where I am from, I would immediately understand that such a person is more interested in where my roots lie. So, I would respond by saying that I am from Britain, but of West African origin. On the other hand, if questioned by a white person, I would stress on the fact that I was born and raised in the United Kingdom, with no reference made to my country of origin. I would only do so if I were further probed by the questioner. The reason for this is that I would not want the questioner to believe that they have any more rights to the claim of being British for the simple fact of them being white and me being black. The situation becomes more complex, however, when referring to children of interracial marriages. In the UK, it is quite common to see a lot of interracial relationships and marriages. When I was growing up in London, I myself knew a few children of parents who were from different racial backgrounds. Sometimes it was difficult for them to affiliate to a particular race when questioned. Did they consider themselves as 'black' or 'white' or just simply 'mixed race'? It all depended on what town or area they grew up in; the ethnic make-up of the school that they had attended; what type of people they had mixed with. If they considered themselves as black, did that mean that they felt British, or Afro-Caribbean (i.e. of Caribbean descent with roots that trace to Africa) or West African of direct African descent? Did they view themselves as being more British if they felt more affiliation to their white parent? What we understand from these questions is that a lot of people in the UK view being British as not only having been born in Britain, but having direct ancestral links to it. The reality therefore is that many of the white British do not actually consider anything other than white as being British, even if such individuals were born in the United Kingdom.

If you were to carry out a survey on the streets of various cities in Britain and ask non-whites at random whether they viewed themselves as being British, you would probably have a majority saying 'yes' even if they were not born there. This is because it is natural to put up a resistance to what may be seen as an attack on one's pride and affiliation. Nobody wants to live in a society in which they perceive that they are being rejected and not wanted, so the natural response would be to challenge such opposition. However, if you were to ask many of the white British if they viewed non-whites as British, you would probably here the complete opposite in the majority of cases, especially if they were asked to be honest in their response. This does not necessarily mean that they are racist, but rather, they just do not feel a sense of pride and honour at having non-whites living amongst them and claiming to be of the same nationality.

The contribution of Ethnic Minority groups to British society

In this section, we will see how this notion, that non-whites cannot really be British, is not always the mainstream viewpoint when it is deemed convenient. The argument of not being truly British unless you are white and can trace your ancestry back to the United Kingdom seems to fall flat on its face when you look at some of the contributions that non-white British citizens have made to their country. In several cases, some of these contributions have been made by individuals who were not even born in Britain, but rendered an honourable service to the country that was worthy of giving them the honour of that affiliation. Let us look at the example of the 2012 and 2016 Olympics in which 'Mo Farah' won both the 5,000 meters and 10,000 meters Olympic gold medals for the long distance track event. Even though he was born and spent his early childhood in Somalia, Britain was so proud of his achievements at the Olympic Games that they would never question his entitlement to British nationality. Whenever they do make reference to his roots, it is only done by way of highlighting his 'rags to riches,' story and it is done with the utmost respect and admiration for his efforts and achievements. In the eyes of the majority of white Britain, Mo Farah is the greatest British athlete of all times and he is British, period! Another example is Rageh Omaar, who was a former BBC World Affairs Correspondent and made his name reporting the Iraq war. Although Rageh was born in Somalia, he is not only considered as

British, but managed to marry into an elite British family. He married Georgiana Rose Montgomery-Cunninghame who is the daughter of Sir John Montgomery-Cunninghame of Corsehill. This family has an elite family tree that traces its lineage all the way back to the 17th century. Not anyone could marry into such a family, not even many of the white British themselves who consider themselves of having a pure lineage. Some of you may have heard of the former British WBC and European heavyweight boxing champion, Frank Bruno. Frank was born in London and is of Caribbean origin. He himself was part of an interracial marriage and he was adored by the British public when he was at his peak. Such was the admiration for him that he was awarded with an MBE (The Most Excellent Order of the British Empire) which is only given by the British monarchy to an individual who has made a significant achievement for the United Kingdom.

White British with non-British ancestry

When it comes to the issue of what makes you British, I mentioned that a person should be able to trace their lineage back to the United Kingdom. They should also be of the white race. However, there are hundreds of thousands of white Britons who have roots elsewhere, yet their affiliation to the UK is never questioned. Sometimes it is possible to identify such individuals by their surnames if you are aware of the origins of such names. In most cases though, you would not normally have had access to such information. The reader may assume I mean that these individuals probably have their roots within other European countries. This is absolutely true in many of the cases. However, there have even been credible scientific studies to suggest that many of the white British actually have <u>West African roots</u>! A study published in the 'New Scientist' magazine on the 24th January 2007 makes the following discovery by stating that,

*"**Gene test on a sample of "indigenous" Englishmen have thrown up a surprise black ancestry, providing new insight into a centuries-old African presence in Britain." (Khamsi, 2007).***

A link to the article can be found online here:

<u>https://www.newscientist.com/article/dn11018-genes-reveal-west-african-heritage-of-white-brits/</u>

The 'Guardian' is a very popular English newspaper and made the following claim in an article published on 18th March 2015, regarding the ancestry of many Britons by mentioning that,

"Genetic study reveals that 30% of white British DNA has German ancestry."

The link to this article can be found online here:

https://www.theguardian.com/science/2015/mar/18/genetic-study-30-percent-white-british-dna-german-ancestry

The following discovery made by the 'Telegraph' newspaper, which is also popular in the UK, is even more alarming. It quotes the following,

"Lord Tebbit, Carol Thatcher and other volunteers thought they were pure Anglo-Saxon – until they were DNA-tested. Andrew Graham watched their jaw drop on discovering racial origins from Africa, the Middle East, even Mongoli. We are all mongrels now, hes says."

See link here:

http://www.telegraph.co.uk/expat/expatfeedback/4201967/So-you-think-youre-English.html

These are just a few examples of some of the alarming discoveries that have been made once we scratch beneath the surface regarding who is really British. The thing is, this information has now been made public, so we should not be allowed to claim ignorance of it anymore. The mere fact that you have at least 30% of white British with German ancestry, or some that have West African, Middle Eastern, or even Mongolian ancestry, should put a lid on this debate of who is British. How far back should your lineage go? Does it not matter just because you are white? If you have German ancestry, should you not then be classed as German according to the definition of some? Where exactly should we draw the line?

It would be really interesting to give DNA tests to members of those white-supremacist political parties in the UK. How would they feel if they found out that their roots actually go back to the Middle East, yet they scream in our faces to go back to our countries?! They propagate their hatred of Islam, Arabs and Muslims, but yet they themselves may well be the descendants of Muslims! What a strange world we live in. What is even more disturbing is that the very same black people that they tell to 'go back to their own countries' may often have white British ancestry as many have discovered! Let us not forget the slave trade and what happened to many black women during that period and the offspring that were produced under illegitimate circumstances. Should such offspring not be given a DNA test on the off chance that they may well be of 'pure' Anglo-Saxon lineage?

How to Deal with Islam and the Muslims

Earlier on, I spoke about the emergence of radical white-supremacist parties. I mentioned that, according to them, a new enemy to British society had been formed – Islam and the Muslims. But is this <u>really</u> the case? Are you <u>not</u> to be considered as being British for the mere fact that you are a practising Muslim? Let us for once ignore all of the media hype and attention surrounding terrorism and atrocities carried out all over the world under the name of Islam. As a Muslim myself, I can never condone any acts of terrorism perpetrated by any group towards another. Let us not forget that <u>blacks</u> were once the focus of attention and the object of oppression both in the United States of America and in the United Kingdom. Yet, blacks were <u>never</u> linked to acts of terrorism. So, why were they being persecuted? Why were they targeted by the very system that was meant to be protecting everyone? Why has there been institutionalised racism in the United Kingdom for decades? What it appears, is that when any group or race is perceived to be a threat to the indigenous population, then it becomes wholly justified to <u>spread fear</u> amongst the masses about such a race or group. Such fears may in many cases be totally unfounded. For example, Muslims from Southern Asia have lived in the United Kingdom for over 60 years now, and they have managed to integrate considerably well into mainstream British society. So why is it <u>now</u>, all of a sudden, that the same community is viewed with deep suspicion and mistrust about where their loyalties and affiliations lie? These Muslims are proud to have built their permanent homes in the United Kingdom and have contributed immensely to the British economy. Are they not therefore worthy of being referred to as British? You have Southern Asian Muslims in all areas and walks of British life, even to the level of law-making. As I write this book, London now has a Muslim mayor. Sadiq Khan did not attain that position as a result of carrying out terrorist acts and taking over by force, but rather, he was actually voted in by Londoners themselves from all walks of life who felt he was representative of their values. In fact, it was during the campaign for mayor that one of his opponents tried to demonize and discredit him due to his religious affiliation. However, his opponent got it terribly wrong and underestimated the voters. London was having none of it. They were not going to buckle in to all of that typical, political smear and scare tactics that is so often hurled around during political campaigns. Instead, London decided to choose hope over fear. Sadiq Khan is a typical example of a proud British citizen who has proven that his religion should not be demonised and used as an excuse to spread fear and hatred amongst the population of Britain. I therefore believe that the Muslims should be left alone to thrive and prosper and contribute positively to British society as opposed to alienating them and viewing them with deep suspicion. Again, I repeat, Sadiq Khan is just one of those examples that his risen to the challenge and has silenced his opponents.

Can real integration really take place in the United Kingdom?

In order for any real integration to occur, the same communities that are now being alienated for their beliefs and practices should be engaged with. Every individual within every community should be made to feel that they are British whatever their religious and political viewpoints are, or whatever their race or ethnic backgrounds are. Being British should not mean that you must adopt other people's opinions and practices, but rather, individuals and communities should be left alone to develop and thrive in the manner in which they see fit. There most definitely has to be tolerance on <u>all</u> sides. Can this not in itself be considered as integration? Should I have to go to my local pub with Joe Bloggs and walk around with a tattoo on my forearms to be considered as British? Should I have to listen to music, and attend concerts and carnivals to be considered as having successfully integrated? Should I have to celebrate religious festivals that have nothing to do with my faith just so that the EDL and UKIP can say, '<u>Now</u> these people are integrating?' If these fundamental values are not upheld, then we are not going to get anywhere. All that we are going to be doing is just further exasperating the situation and polarising the already alienated communities.

To conclude, Britain has always had an open-door policy to immigration and a level of tolerance unparalleled in Europe.

However, all of its citizens need to have a strong sense of belonging. They have to feel that their claim to being British should never be scrutinized under the microscope. There should be no groups or political parties that are allowed to intimidate others for just merely being different. Nobody is saying that you should 'love thy neighbour', but you should definitely try to look out for their well-being. It is so easy to spread hate and mistrust within communities, but it takes huge effort to build bridges and spread peace. When we take a look around the world, we clearly see the results of what happens when hate-mongering is kept unchecked. The United States of America is coming under heavy criticism and scrutiny because of its failure to deal with the recent incidences of police brutality directed at a community that no-one could ever have doubt about their legitimate claim to being American. So what do we think will happen if hate-speech is allowed to continue in the way it is happening in the United Kingdom right now? Is this something we really want to be seeing on the streets of Britain? This is all because we do not want to see the 'other' as really being 'British'. This is clearly not a 'white and black' issue.

www.ingramcontent.com/pod-product-compliance
Lightning Source LLC
Chambersburg PA
CBHW030551290526
45786CB00004B/1977